Forty Hours Devotion

EUCHARISTIC ADORATION

A Redemptorist Pastoral Publication

Liguori
PUBLICATIONS
A Redemptorist Ministry

Catholic. Pastoral. Trusted.

Imprimi Potest: Kevin Zubel, CSsR, Provincial
Denver Province, the Redemptorists

Published by Liguori Publications, Liguori, Missouri 63057

Liguori Publications, a nonprofit corporation, is an apostolate of the Redemptorists (Redemptorists.com).
Phone: 800-325-9521 Web: Liguori.org

Forty Hours: Eucharistic Adoration
A Redemptorist Pastoral Publication

ISBN 978-0-7648-2873-7
E-ISBN: 978-0-7648-7256-3

Cataloging-in-Publication data has been applied for with the Library of Congress

Note: Some of the prayers and text contained here are adapted from the previously published book *Eucharistic Devotion: Renewing a Timeless Tradition*, a Redemptorist Pastoral Publication, Liguori Publications (808425), 2002.

Printed in the United States of America
29 28 27 26 25 / 5 4 3 2 1
First Edition

Cover design: Wendy Barnes
Cover photo: Stock Studio/Shutterstock

Contents

"I urge you to devote yourselves in particular to prayer of adoration: this is important. Today, the meaning of prayer of adoration, of spending time in worship, has been somewhat lost. This prayer is not often done; I ask you to do it. To worship, to immerse yourselves in divine love and give it to those you meet on your path. It is beautiful to worship in silence before the Blessed Sacrament, to be in the consoling presence of Jesus and there to draw the apostolic impetus to be instruments of goodness, tenderness, and welcome in the community, in the Church, and in the world."

Pope Francis, October 22, 2022
Address to the participants in the General Chapters of the Order of the Most Holy Savior of Saint Bridget and the Comboni Missionary Sisters

"If we really loved the good God, we should make it our joy and happiness to come and spend a few moments to adore him and ask him for the grace of forgiveness, and we should regard those moments as the happiest of our lives."

Saint John Vianney (1786–1859)

"I adore you, and I thank you for all the graces you have bestowed on me, especially for having given me yourself in this sacrament, for having given me your most holy Mother, Mary, to plead for me, and for having called me to visit you in this church."

Saint Alphonsus Liguori (1696–1787)

Section One

Celebration of the Forty Hours Devotion

The Roman Ritual *Holy Communion and Worship of the Eucharist Outside Mass* states, "In churches where the Eucharist is regularly reserved, it is recommended that solemn exposition of the Blessed Sacrament for an extended period should take place once a year, even though this period is not strictly continuous. In this way, the local community may reflect more profoundly upon this mystery and adore Christ in the sacrament."

In the document *The Mystery of the Eucharist in the Life of the Church*, the United States Conference of Catholic Bishops (USCCB) says, "We rejoice in the growing numbers of the faithful who pray in adoration before the Blessed Sacrament, a testament of faith in the Real Presence of the Lord in the Eucharist. We encourage this devotion, which helps all of us to be formed by the self-giving love we behold in the Lord's gift of himself in the Eucharist."

The instructions that follow include the liturgical norms and guidelines for the Forty Hours devotion outlined in the *Order for Solemn Exposition of the Eucharist*, published by the USCCB in 1993. The content provided here is adapted from those guidelines.

Opening Mass

The Forty Hours devotion opens with the celebration of Mass, for "the celebration of the Eucharist in the sacrifice of the Mass is the origin and consummation of the worship shown to the Eucharist outside Mass" (*Eucharisticum Mysterium*, 3e).

Exposition

During or at the conclusion of the Communion Rite of Mass, the ministers and altar servers prepare the altar for exposition of the Blessed Sacrament. Traditionally, the altar is adorned with four to six lighted candles. The monstrance is placed on the altar. At the conclusion of the distribution of Communion, the celebrant says the prayer after Communion. The celebrant then places the host, which has been consecrated at Mass, in the monstrance. He positions the monstrance on the altar to face the people, then incenses the holy Eucharist in the monstrance while a traditional hymn is sung.

At the conclusion of the hymn and the incensation, the celebrant and altar servers depart the sanctuary. There is no final blessing or dismissal at this Mass.

Hymn—Traditionally Sung During Exposition

"O Salutaris Hostia"

Latin	**English**
O salutaris Hostia	O Victim bringing saving grace,
Quae caeli pandis ostium:	who opens wide the gate of heav'n:
Bella premunt hostilia,	our foes assail and press us hard;
Da robur, fer auxilium.	give us your strength, bring us your aid.
Uni trinoque Domino	To you be everlasting praise
Sit sempiterna gloria,	and glory, One and Triune Lord,
Qui vitam sine termino	who grants us life that knows no end,
Nobis donet in patria.	for ever in our heav'nly home.
Amen.	Amen.

Adoration

Adoration of the most holy Eucharist takes place for the remainder of the period of public prayer, interrupted only for the celebration of daily Mass. The host is removed from the monstrance and returned to the tabernacle before daily Mass begins. When Mass concludes, the host is placed once again in the monstrance, and exposition continues.

Exposition is "intended to acknowledge Christ's marvelous presence in the sacrament" and "invites us to the spiritual union with him that culminates in sacramental Communion" (*Holy Communion and Worship of the Eucharist Outside Mass*).

Public Prayers

During the period of public exposition, there is opportunity for public prayer. The format of prayers selected for this purpose allows for a variety of liturgical choices. See Section Two for options.

Proclamation of the Word/Preaching

It is appropriate during exposition to proclaim the word of God and offer a fitting sermon that celebrates the holy Eucharist. Traditionally, the proclamation of the word and the preaching that follows is supported by a liturgical service that has been prepared for this purpose. See Section Two for options.

Benediction

When the designated forty-hour period of exposition has concluded, the devotion closes with solemn Benediction, in which the church, joined in prayer, is blessed with the Body of Christ. This service is celebrated before the closing Solemn Mass, and it formally ends the Forty Hours devotion. When possible, it is preferred to celebrate a closing Mass of Thanksgiving directly following Benediction.

Hymn—Traditionally Sung During Benediction

"Tantum Ergo Sacramentum"

Latin	**English**
Tantum ergo Sacramentum	Let us, therefore, bow and worship
Veneremur cernui:	such a wondrous Sacrament;
Et antiquum Documentum	let the ancient law and custom
Novo cedat ritui:	to a newer rite now yield;
Præstet fides supplementum	let our faith supply conviction
Sensuum defectui.	where the senses tire and fail.
Genitori, Genitoque	To the Father, unbegotten,
Laus et jubilatio,	and the Sole-begotten Son,
Salus, honor, virtus quoque	be salvation, blessing, honor,
Sit et benedictio:	jubilation, pow'r, and praise;
Procedenti ab utroque	to the One from both proceeding
Compar sit laudatio.	equal glory and renown.
Amen.	Amen.

Verse and Prayer

Celebrant: Let us pray. O God, who in this wonderful Sacrament have left us a memorial of your Passion, grant us, we pray, so to revere the sacred mysteries of your Body and Blood that we may always experience in ourselves the fruits of your redemption. Who live and reign, for ever and ever. Amen.

Divine Praises

Blessed be God.
Blessed be his holy Name.
Blessed be Jesus Christ, true God and true man.
Blessed be the Name of Jesus.
Blessed be his most Sacred Heart.

Blessed be his most Precious Blood.
Blessed be Jesus in the most holy Sacrament of the altar.
Blessed be the Holy Spirit, the Paraclete.
Blessed be the great Mother of God, Mary most holy.
Blessed be her holy and Immaculate Conception.
Blessed be her glorious Assumption.
Blessed be the name of Mary, Virgin and Mother.
Blessed be St. Joseph, her most chaste Spouse.
Blessed be God in his Angels and in his Saints.

May the heart of Jesus, in the most Blessed Sacrament, be praised, adored, and loved with grateful affection, at every moment, in all the tabernacles of the world, even to the end of time. Amen.

Hymn—Reposition of the Blessed Sacrament

"Holy God, We Praise Thy Name"

Verse 1
Holy God, we praise thy name;
Lord of all, we bow before thee!
All on earth thy scepter claim,
All in heaven above adore thee;
Infinite, thy vast domain,
Everlasting is thy reign.

Verse 2
Hark! the loud celestial hymn
Angel choirs above are raising;
Cherubim and Seraphim,
In unceasing chorus praising;
Fill the heavens with sweet accord:
"Holy, holy, holy Lord!"

Hymns for Adoration and Benediction

Latin

"Adoro Te Devote"
"In Splendoribus Sanctorum"
"O Salutaris Hostia"
"Pange Lingua"
"Panis Angelicus"
"Tantum Ergo Sacramentum"
"Ubi Caritas"
"Adoramus Te Domine" by Taizé

English Traditional

"Holy God, We Praise Thy Name"
"How Great Thou Art"
"Jesus, My Lord, My God, My All"
"Let All Mortal Flesh Keep Silence"
"O God of Loveliness"
"O Radiant Light"
"The King of Love My Shepherd Is"
"O Sacrament Most Holy"
"I Received the Living God"

English Contemporary

"Shepherd of Souls" by James Montgomery and John B. Dykes
"Bread of Life" by Bobby Fisher
"For All Once Broken" by James Quinn, SJ, and Steve Angrisano
"I Am the Bread of Life" by Suzanne Toolan, RSM
"God Be in My Head" by Grayson Warren Brown
"Sanctuary" by John Thompson and Randy Scruggs
"Take, O Take Me As I Am" by John Bell

English Gospel

"Catch Me Singing" by Sean Curran

"Christ Be Magnified" by Cody Carnes, Cory Asbury, and Ethan Hulse

"Easy to Praise" by Patrick Mayberry

"First Love" by Kari Jobe

"Goodness of God" by Bethel Music and Jenn Johnson

"How Deep the Father's Love" by Church of the City

"How Great Is Our God" by Chris Tomlin

"Savior of the World" by Mack Brock

"The House of God, Forever" by Jon Foreman

Spanish

"Holy Forever" (Español) by Chris Tomlin and Miel San Marcos

"Vasijas Rotas" (Sublime Gracia) by Hillsong Worship

"Cuán Grande Es Dios" by En Espíritu Y En Verdad

"Mi Esperanza Está en Jesús" by Bethel Music

"Incontrolable Amor" by Christine D'Clario

"Alaba" by Elevation Worship, Elevation Español, and Unified Sound

"Con Todo Mi Ser" by Leeland and Majo y Dan

"Gloria A Cristo" by Bethany Wohrle and Bethel Music

"Gracia Sublime Es" by Phil Wickham

"Mismo Dios" by Elevation Worship

"Quien Dices Que Soy" by Hillsong Worship

"Rey de Reyes" by Hillsong Worship and Hillsong En Español

"Rindo Mis Coronas" by Gateway Worship Español

Section Two

Alternative Formats of the Forty Hours Devotion for Congregational Use

FORMAT ONE

Prayer of Preparation

Celebrant: O Lord, give me the words to adequately praise your holy presence in the eucharistic sacrament. Remove from me the spirit of pride and resistance to your will for me. Cleanse me of every sin of body and spirit. Purify my heart of all distractions, worldly concerns, and sinful thoughts. Give me also the grace to understand, and the will to proceed worthily, so that I may pray to you with attentive devotion before your eternal Majesty. I pray this through our Lord Jesus Christ, your Son, who lives and reigns with you and the Holy Spirit, for ever and ever. Amen.

Hymn

"Pange Lingua Gloriosi" by St. Thomas Aquinas
Translated by Edward Caswall (1814–1878)

Verse 1
Sing, my tongue, the Savior's glory,
Of his flesh the myst'ry sing;
Of the Blood, all price exceeding,
Shed by our immortal King,
Destined for the world's redemption,
From a noble womb to spring.

Verse 2
Of a pure and spotless virgin
Born for us on earth below,
He, as man with man conversing,
Stayed the seeds of truth to sow;
Then he closed in solemn order
Wondrously his life of woe.

Verse 3
On the night of that last supper,
Seated with his chosen band,
He, the paschal victim eating,
First fulfills the law's command;
Then as food to his apostles
Gives himself with his own hand.

Verse 4
Word made flesh,
the bread of nature
By his word to flesh he turns;
Wine into his Blood he changes:
What though sense no change
discerns?
Only be the heart in earnest,
Faith her lesson quickly learns.

Verse 5
Down in adoration falling,
Lo! the sacred Host we hail;
Lo! o'er ancient forms departing,
newer rites of grace prevail;
faith for all defects supplying,
where the feeble sense fail.

Verse 6
To the everlasting Father,
And the Son who reigns on high,
With the Holy Spirit proceeding
Forth from each eternally,
Be salvation, honor, blessing,
Might and endless majesty.

Prayer

Lector: Come, let us praise the Lord with joyful hearts. Let us sing joyfully to God our Savior. Let us pray in his presence with thankfulness and let us make joyful noise to him with all our being. Amen.

First Eucharistic Scripture Reading

1 Corinthians 11:17–27

Lector: A reading from the first Letter of St. Paul to the Corinthians.

Brothers and sisters: In giving this instruction, I do not praise the fact that your meetings are doing more harm than good. First of all, I hear that when you meet as a Church there are divisions among you, and to a degree I believe it; there have to be factions among you in order that also those who are approved among you may become known. When you meet in one place, then, it is not to eat the Lord's supper, for in eating, each one goes ahead with his own supper, and one goes hungry while another gets drunk. Do you not have houses in which you can eat and drink? Or do you show contempt for the Church of God and make those who have nothing feel ashamed? What can I say to you? Shall I praise you? In this matter I do not praise you.

For I received from the Lord what I also handed on to you, that the Lord Jesus, on the night he was handed over, took bread, and, after he had given thanks, broke it and said, "This is my Body that is for you. Do this in remembrance of me." In the same way also the cup, after supper, saying, "This cup is the new covenant in my Blood. Do this, as often as you drink it, in remembrance of me." For as often as you eat this bread and drink the cup, you proclaim the death of the Lord until he comes.

Lector: The word of the Lord.
All: **Thanks be to God.**

Responsorial

Psalm 147:1–2, 3–4, 5–6

R. Praise the LORD, who heals the brokenhearted.

Praise the LORD, for he is good;
sing praise to our God, for he is gracious;
it is fitting to praise him.
The LORD rebuilds Jerusalem;
the dispersed of Israel he gathers.

R. Praise the LORD, who heals the brokenhearted.

He heals the brokenhearted
and binds up their wounds.
He tells the number of the stars;
he calls each by name.

R. Praise the LORD, who heals the brokenhearted.

Great is our LORD and mighty in power;
to his wisdom there is no limit.
The LORD sustains the lowly;
the wicked he casts to the ground.

R. Praise the LORD, who heals the brokenhearted.

Prayer

Celebrant: O Father, giver of your Son and of every good thing, give us bread for our physical well-being, and give us the nourishment of your word and of your doctrine for our spiritual strength. We ask this through Christ, our Lord. Amen.

Second Eucharistic Scripture Reading

John 6:51–58

Celebrant: The Lord be with you.
All: **And with your spirit.**
Celebrant: A reading from the holy Gospel according to John.
All: **Glory to you, O Lord.**

[Jesus said to the crowds,]
"I am the living bread that came down from heaven;
whoever eats this bread will live forever;
and the bread that I will give
is my Flesh for the life of the world."

The Jews quarreled among themselves, saying,
"How can this man give us [his] flesh to eat?"
Jesus said to them,
"Amen, amen, I say to you,
unless you eat the Flesh of the Son of Man and drink his Blood,
you do not have life within you.

Whoever eats my Flesh and drinks my Blood
has eternal life,
and I will raise him on the last day.
For my Flesh is true food,
and my Blood is true drink.
Whoever eats my Flesh and drinks my Blood
remains in me and I in him.

Just as the living Father sent me
and I have life because of the Father,
so also the one who feeds on me
will have life because of me.

This is the bread that came down from heaven.
Unlike your ancestors who ate and still died,
whoever eats this bread will live forever."

Celebrant: The Gospel of the Lord.
All: **Praise to you, Lord Jesus Christ.**

Prayer

Celebrant: United with Christ in the bond of the Eucharist, we keep watch here in faithful love of you, our Father. We have come to offer adoration to your Son, who lays down his human life for us and our salvation. May our prayers lead us to the light of eternal life, even as the star led the Magi to your infant Son in the stable. We ask this through Christ, our Lord. Amen.

If a sermon is to be preached, it should follow the Scripture readings and the prayer. If there is no sermon, an extended period of silence follows. The optional Eucharistic Meditation below provides appropriate points for reflection and prayer. It should be read by the lector if no sermon is preached.

Eucharistic Meditation *by St. Thérèse of Lisieux*

Lector: Do you realize that Jesus is there in the tabernacle expressly for you—for you alone? He burns with the desire to come into your heart.... Don't listen to the demon, laugh at him, and go without fear to receive the Jesus of peace and love....

Receive Communion often, very often.... There you have the sole remedy, if you want to be cured. Jesus has not put this attraction into your heart for nothing.... The guest of our soul knows our misery; he comes to find an empty tent within us—that is all he asks.

Prayers of Intercession

You graciously give to your people the bread of life. We ask that you bring us out of the death caused by sin. To the Lord of all life, we pray:
R. As we eat this bread and drink this cup, we proclaim your death and resurrection, Lord Jesus.

You give us hope from the supper your Son gave to us in this world. May we find contentment in this meal we share. To the Lord of all life, we pray:
R. As we eat this bread and drink this cup, we proclaim your death and resurrection, Lord Jesus.

You give us love through the blood your Son poured out for us. May we be washed clean of all our sins. To the Lord of all life, we pray:
R. As we eat this bread and drink this cup, we proclaim your death and resurrection, Lord Jesus.

You give to the world the promise of life eternal. We ask that you claim for your own all those who have died. To the Lord of all life, we pray:
R. As we eat this bread and drink this cup, we proclaim your death and resurrection, Lord Jesus.

Litany of Praise to the Holy Name of Jesus

Lord, have mercy on us. **Christ, have mercy on us.**
Lord, have mercy on us. Jesus, hear us. **Jesus, graciously hear us.**

God the Father of heaven, **have mercy on us.**
God the Son, Redeemer of the world, **have mercy on us.**
God the Holy Spirit, **have mercy on us.**
Holy Trinity, one God, **have mercy on us.**

Jesus, Son of the living God, **have mercy on us.**
Jesus, Splendor of the Father, **have mercy on us.**
Jesus, Brightness of eternal light, **have mercy on us.**
Jesus, King of glory, **have mercy on us.**
Jesus, Sun of justice, **have mercy on us.**
Jesus, Son of the Virgin Mary, **have mercy on us.**
Jesus, most amiable, **have mercy on us.**
Jesus, most admirable, **have mercy on us.**
Jesus, mighty God, **have mercy on us.**

Jesus, Father of the world to come, **have mercy on us.**

Jesus, Angel of great counsel, **have mercy on us.**

Jesus, most powerful, **have mercy on us.**

Jesus, most patient, **have mercy on us.**

Jesus, most obedient, **have mercy on us.**

Jesus, meek and humble of heart, **have mercy on us.**

Jesus, Lover of chastity, **have mercy on us.**

Jesus, Lover of us, **have mercy on us.**

Jesus, God of peace, **have mercy on us.**

Jesus, Author of life, **have mercy on us.**

Jesus, Model of all virtues, **have mercy on us.**

Jesus, zealous Lover of souls, **have mercy on us.**

Jesus, our God, **have mercy on us.**

Jesus, our Refuge, **have mercy on us.**

Jesus, Father of the poor, **have mercy on us.**

Jesus, true Light, **have mercy on us.**

Jesus, eternal Wisdom, **have mercy on us.**

Jesus, good Shepherd, **have mercy on us.**

Jesus, infinite Goodness, **have mercy on us.**

Jesus, Treasure of the faithful, **have mercy on us.**

Jesus, our Way and our Life, **have mercy on us.**

Jesus, Joy of angels, **have mercy on us.**

Jesus, King of patriarchs, **have mercy on us.**

Jesus, Master of apostles, **have mercy on us.**

Jesus, Teacher of evangelists, **have mercy on us.**

Jesus, Strength of martyrs, **have mercy on us.**

Jesus, Light of confessors, **have mercy on us.**

Jesus, Purity of virgins, **have mercy on us.**

Jesus, Crown of all saints, **have mercy on us.**

Be merciful, spare us, O Jesus.

Be merciful, graciously hear us, O Jesus.

From all evil, **O Jesus, deliver us.**

From all sin, **O Jesus, deliver us.**

From your wrath, **O Jesus, deliver us.**

From the snares of the devil, **O Jesus, deliver us.**

From everlasting death, **O Jesus, deliver us.**

From the neglect of your inspirations, **O Jesus, deliver us.**

Through the mystery of your Incarnation, **O Jesus, deliver us.**

Through your Nativity, **O Jesus, deliver us.**

Through your Infancy, **O Jesus, deliver us.**

Through your most divine life, **O Jesus, deliver us.**

Through your labors, **O Jesus, deliver us.**

Through your agony and passion, **O Jesus, deliver us.**

Through your cross, **O Jesus, deliver us.**

Through your death and burial, **O Jesus, deliver us.**

Through your resurrection, **O Jesus, deliver us.**

Through your ascension, **O Jesus, deliver us.**

Through your institution of the most holy Eucharist,
O Jesus, deliver us.

Through your joys, **O Jesus, deliver us.**

Through your glory, **O Jesus, deliver us.**

Lamb of God, who takes away the sins of the world,
spare us, O Jesus.

Lamb of God, who takes away the sins of the world,
have mercy on us, O Jesus.

Jesus, hear us. **Jesus, graciously hear us. Amen.**

Closing Hymn

An appropriate closing hymn is sung as the celebrant, lector, and other ministers leave the altar.

Format Two / During Easter Season

Prayer of Preparation *from the Armenian Liturgy*

Celebrant: Let us witness the holiness of the most pure Body and Blood of our Lord and Savior Jesus Christ, who, having descended from heaven, is distributed among us. He is the Life, the Hope, the Resurrection, the Cleansing, and the Remission of sins. Amen.

Lector: Sing a psalm to our immortal, heavenly King, who sits on the chariot of the Cherubim. Sing a psalm to the Lord, O you Choirs. Sing to him in a sweet voice, for the psalms, and their melodies, are fitting for him. You his ministers praise the Lord in the heavens, for Christ is brought and distributed to us here on earth. Alleluia.

He gives us his Body for our food, and washes us with his holy Blood, alleluia. Come near to the Lord, and receive his light, alleluia. Taste and see how good the Lord is, alleluia. Bless the Lord in the heavens, alleluia. Bless him in the highest, alleluia. Bless him all you his angels, alleluia.

Hymn

"Shepherd of Souls" by James Montgomery (1771–1854)

Shepherd of souls, refresh and bless
Your chosen pilgrim flock
With manna in the wilderness,
With water from the rock.

Hungry and thirsty, faint and weak,
As you when here below,
Our souls the joys celestial seek
Which from your sorrows flow.

We would not live by bread alone,
But by your word of grace,
In strength of which we travel on
To our abiding place.

Prayer

Celebrant: Come, O Lord our God, from your throne of glory in your kingdom. Come and sanctify us, you who sit above with the Father, but who is here invisibly present with us. Come and help us give worthy thanks to you for all the gifts which you have lavished on us. You who have given us these gifts, allow us to be faithful witnesses to your Real Presence in the holy Eucharist and let us be united to your Body and Blood, so that you may dwell in our hearts. We ask this in your holy name. Amen.

First Eucharistic Scripture Reading

Hebrews 9:11–15

Lector: A reading from the Letter to the Hebrews.

Brothers and sisters:
When Christ came as high priest
of the good things that have come to be,
passing through the greater and more perfect tabernacle
not made by hands, that is, not belonging to this creation,
he entered once for all into the sanctuary,
not with the blood of goats and calves
but with his own blood, thus obtaining eternal redemption.

For if the blood of goats and bulls
and the sprinkling of a heifer's ashes
can sanctify those who are defiled
so that their flesh is cleansed,
how much more will the Blood of Christ,

who through the eternal Spirit offered himself unblemished to God,
cleanse our consciences from dead works
to worship the living God.

For this reason, he is mediator of a new covenant:
since a death has taken place for deliverance
from transgressions under the first covenant,
those who are called may receive the promised eternal inheritance.

Lector: The word of the Lord.
***All:* Thanks be to God.**

Responsorial

Psalm 81:3–4, 5–6, 7–8, 10–11

R. Sing with joy to God our help.

Take up a melody, and sound the timbrel,
the pleasant harp and the lyre.
Blow the trumpet at the new moon,
at the full moon, on our solemn feast.

R. Sing with joy to God our help.

For it is a statute in Israel,
an ordinance of the God of Jacob,
who made it a decree for Joseph
when he came forth from the land of Egypt.

R. Sing with joy to God our help.

An unfamiliar speech I hear:
"I relieved his shoulder of the burden;
his hands were freed from the basket.
In distress you called, and I rescued you."

R. Sing with joy to God our help.

"There shall be no strange god among you
nor shall you worship any alien god.
I, the Lord, am your God
who led you forth from the land of Egypt."

R. Sing with joy to God our help.

Prayer

Celebrant: Lord God, you who have sent your Son to establish the new and perfect covenant which binds us intimately to you, grant that the Blood of Christ may be an everlasting source of life for us. May we always acknowledge this source of life, through which we have been redeemed; may this Blood be a sign of faith in your promises. Through Christ, our Lord. Amen.

Second Eucharistic Scripture Reading

Acts of the Apostles 2:42–47

Lector: A reading from the Acts of the Apostles.

The brothers and sisters devoted themselves to the teaching of the Apostles and to the communal life, to the breaking of the bread and to the prayers. Awe came upon everyone, and many wonders and signs were done through the Apostles. All who believed were together and had all things in common; they would sell their property and possessions and divide them among all according to each one's need. Every day they devoted themselves to meeting together in the temple area and to breaking bread in their homes. They ate their meals with exultation and sincerity of heart, praising God and enjoying favor with all the people. And every day the Lord added to their number those who were being saved.

Lector: The word of the Lord.
All: **Thanks be to God.**

Prayer

Celebrant: Make us truly a eucharistic community, Lord, aware of the source that gives life to each of us and trustful of the certainty of your eternal love. Let us stretch out our hands to each other and to all those in need of your hope, your help, and your healing. Through Christ, our Lord. Amen.

If a sermon is to be preached, it should follow the Scripture readings and the prayer. If there is no sermon, an extended period of silence follows. The optional Eucharistic Meditation below provides appropriate points for reflection and prayer. It should be read by the lector if no sermon is preached.

Eucharistic Meditation

by Pope St. John Paul II, World Youth Day Homily, August 24, 1997

Lector: "Rabbi, where are you staying?" Each day the Church responds: Christ is present in the Eucharist, in the sacrament of his death and resurrection. In and through the Eucharist, you acknowledge the dwelling-place of the living God in human history. For the Eucharist is the sacrament of the love which conquers death; it is the sacrament of the Covenant, pure gift of love for the reconciliation of all humanity. It is the gift of the Real Presence of Jesus the Redeemer, in the bread which is his Body given up for us, in the wine which is his Blood poured out for all. Thanks to the Eucharist, constantly renewed among all peoples of the world, Christ continues to build his Church: he brings us together in praise and thanksgiving for salvation, in the communion which only infinite love can forge.... May your presence here mean a true commitment in faith! For Christ is now answering your own question and the questions of all those who seek the living God. He answers by offering an invitation: this is my Body, take it and eat. To the Father he entrusts his supreme desire: that all those whom he loves may be one in the same communion.

Prayers of Intercession

Help us to be a community of peace, for if we are not peaceful ourselves, we cannot create peace in others. To the Lord of all life we pray:

R. Send us your light, your peace, and your presence that conquers all hatred and anger.

Help us renew our efforts to be peaceful to all we meet during the day, for you can bring order and love to the most ordinary of circumstances. To the Lord of all life we pray:

R. Send us your light, your peace, and your presence that conquers all hatred and anger.

Help us participate in true peace, not in cease-fires, not in armed truces, nor in silent and resentful tolerance, for only you, the Prince of Peace, can bring us peace that passes all understanding. To the Lord of all life we pray:

R. Send us your light, your peace, and your presence that conquers all hatred and anger.

Offer us your assurances that those who have gone before us will find peace everlasting with you in heaven. To the Lord of all life we pray:

R. Send us your light, your peace, and your presence as we travel on our own salvation journey and eventually rejoice with you and the communion of saints in the perfect peace of your heavenly home.

Litany of Praise for the Blessed Sacrament

Lord, have mercy on us. **Christ, have mercy on us.**
Lord, have mercy on us. Christ, hear us. **Christ graciously hear us.**

God, the Father of Heaven, **have mercy on us.**
God, the Son, Redeemer of the world, **have mercy on us.**
Holy Trinity, one God, **have mercy on us.**

Living Bread that came down from heaven, **have mercy on us.**
Hidden God and Savior, **have mercy on us.**
Wheat and Wine of the elect, **have mercy on us.**
Bread of abundance, **have mercy on us.**
Perpetual Sacrifice, **have mercy on us.**
Clean Oblation, **have mercy on us.**
Lamb without spot, **have mercy on us.**
Most pure Feast, **have mercy on us.**
Food of angels, **have mercy on us.**
Hidden Manna, **have mercy on us.**
Memorial of the wonders of God, **have mercy on us.**
Supersubstantial Bread, **have mercy on us.**
Word made flesh, dwelling in us, **have mercy on us.**
Sacred Host, **have mercy on us.**
Chalice of benediction, **have mercy on us.**
Mystery of faith, **have mercy on us.**
Most holy of all Sacrifices, **have mercy on us.**
Heavenly Antidote against the poison of sin, **have mercy on us.**
Most wonderful of all Miracles, **have mercy on us.**
Holy Commemoration of the passion of Christ, **have mercy on us.**
Memorial of divine love, **have mercy on us.**
Overflowing of divine bounty, **have mercy on us.**
Medicine of immortality, **have mercy on us.**
Live-giving Sacrament, **have mercy on us.**
Bread made flesh by the power of the Word, **have mercy on us.**

Unbloody Sacrifice, **have mercy on us.**
At once our Feast and our Guest, **have mercy on us.**
Bond of charity, **have mercy on us.**
Priest and Victim, **have mercy on us.**
Refreshment of holy souls, **have mercy on us.**
Pledge of future glory, **have mercy on us.**

Be merciful, **spare us, O Lord.**
Be merciful, **graciously hear us, O Lord.**

From an unworthy reception of your Body and Blood,
O Lord, deliver us.

From the pride of life, **O Lord, deliver us.**

From every occasion of sin, **O Lord, deliver us.**

Through the desire with which you longed to eat this Passover with your disciples, **O Lord, deliver us.**

Through the humility with which you washed their feet,
O Lord, deliver us.

Through the love by which you instituted this divine sacrament,
O Lord, deliver us.

Through your precious Blood, which you did leave upon our altars,
O Lord, deliver us.

Through the five wounds of this your most holy Body,
O Lord, deliver us.

We sinners beseech you, hear us, that you will preserve and increase our faith, and devotion toward this sacrament,
we beseech you, hear us.

That you will conduct us, through true confession of our sins, to a frequent reception of the holy Eucharist,
we beseech you, hear us.

That you will deliver us from all unfaithfulness and blindness of heart, **we beseech you, hear us.**

That you will grant to us the heavenly fruits of this most holy sacrament, **we beseech you, hear us.**

That at the hour of our death you will strengthen and defend us by this heavenly viaticum, **we beseech you, hear us.**

Son of God, **we beseech you, hear us.**

Lamb of God, who takes away the sins of the world,
spare us, O Lord.

Lamb of God, who takes away the sins of the world,
graciously hear us, O Lord.

Lamb of God, who takes away the sins of the world,
have mercy on us.

Celebrant: Let us pray. O God, who in this sacrament has left us a memorial of your passion, grant us the grace, we ask of you, so to venerate the sacred mysteries of your Body and Blood, that we may ever continue to feel within ourselves the blessed fruit of your redemption, who lives and reigns, God, forever and ever. Amen.

Closing Hymn

An appropriate closing hymn is sung as the celebrant, lector, and other ministers leave the altar.

Section Three

Alternative Formats of the Forty Hours Devotion for Private Prayer

Prayer of Preparation

O God, who made the seas and the dry lands, the stars and the sun, let us come and adore you in your most sacred mystery of the Eucharist. Let us fall down on our knees before you and let us weep for our sins in the presence of the Lord who made us, for you are our Lord, and we are your people. Amen.

Hail Mary...

Our Father...

Hymn

"At the Lamb's High Feast We Sing"

"Ad Regias Agni Dapes" (Fourth Century), Translated by Robert Campbell (1814–1868)

At the Lamb's high feast we sing,
Praise to our victorious King,
Who hath washed us in the tide
Flowing from his pierced side;

Praise we him, whose love divine
Gives his sacred Blood for wine,
Gives his Body for the feast,
Christ the Victim, Christ the Priest.

Where the Paschal Blood is poured,
Death's dark angel sheathes his sword;
Israel's hosts triumphant go
Through the wave that drowns the foe.
Praise we Christ, whose Blood was shed,
Paschal Victim, Paschal Bread;
With sincerity and love
Eat we manna from above.

Prayer

With confidence, we pray to the Lamb of God that this time spent in prayer in front of your eucharistic presence will be a fruitful effort. You, the Lamb of God, who protected your people from the angel of death, mark the doors of our hearts with your saving Blood. Bring us and all our beloved dead to your wedding feast in heaven, where all is praise and rejoicing. Amen.

Responsorial

Psalm 23:1–3, 4, 5, 6

R. The Lord is my shepherd; there is nothing I shall want.

The Lord is my shepherd; I shall not want.
In verdant pastures he gives me repose;
Beside restful waters he leads me;
he refreshes my soul.

R. The Lord is my shepherd; there is nothing I shall want.

He guides me in right paths for his name's sake.

Even though I walk in the dark valley
I fear no evil; for you are at my side
With your rod and your staff
that give me courage.

R. The LORD is my shepherd; there is nothing I shall want.

You spread the table before me
in the sight of my foes;
You anoint my head with oil;
my cup overflows.

R. The LORD is my shepherd; there is nothing I shall want.

Only goodness and kindness follow me
all the days of my life;
And I shall dwell in the house of the LORD
for years to come.

R. The LORD is my shepherd; there is nothing I shall want.

First Eucharistic Scripture Reading

Mark 14:12–16, 22–26

On the first day of the Feast of Unleavened Bread, when they sacrificed the Passover Lamb, Jesus' disciples said to him, "Where do you want us to go and prepare for you to eat the Passover?" He sent two of his disciples and said to them, "Go into the city, and a man will meet you, carrying a jar of water. Follow him. Wherever he enters, say to the master of the house, 'The Teacher says, "Where is my guest room where I may eat the Passover with my disciples?"' Then he will show you a large upper room, furnished and ready. Make the preparations for us there." The disciples then went off, entered the city, and found it just as he had told them; and they prepared the Passover.

While they were eating, he took bread, said the blessing, broke it, and gave it to them, and said, "Take it; this is my Body." Then he took a cup, gave thanks, and gave it to them, and they all drank from it. He said to them, "This is my Blood of the covenant, which will be shed for many. Amen, I say to you, I shall not drink again the fruit of the vine until the day when I drink it new in the kingdom of God." Then, after singing a hymn, they went out to the Mount of Olives.

Prayer

Holy Lord and Father, you gather us around the table of your Son, who was given for our salvation. Grant that we may not fall prey to the lure of earthly goods nor participate in the shortsighted quest for successes in this life, but may your Son bring us enlightenment so that we may discern the passing from the eternal, the true from the false. Through Christ, our Lord. Amen.

Second Eucharistic Scripture Reading

John 6:30–35

The crowd said to Jesus, "What sign can you do, that we may see and believe in you? What can you do? Our ancestors ate manna in the desert, as it is written:

He gave them bread from heaven to eat."

So Jesus said to them, "Amen, amen, I say to you, it was not Moses who gave the bread from heaven; my Father gives you the true bread from heaven. For the bread of God is that which comes down from heaven and gives life to the world."

So they said to Jesus, "Sir, give us this bread always." Jesus said to them, "I am the bread of life; whoever comes to me will never hunger, and whoever believes in me will never thirst."

Prayer

Father of Mercy, whose Son resisted the temptation to transform stones into bread, strengthen our desire to avoid all temptation. Father of Mercy, whose Son Jesus left the bread and wine as a remembrance of him, grant that we who pray before the Blessed Sacrament may be a sign to all of his great promise of life and true liberation.

We ask this through Christ, our Lord. Amen.

Eucharistic Meditation

The Imitation of Christ, Book 4, Part 1, by Thomas à Kempis

Many people make pilgrimages to distant places to venerate the relics of the saints, where, hearing with wonder the report of their miracles and gazing in awe at the magnificent churches erected in their honor, they kiss these sacred bones enshrined in golden reliquaries. Yet right here with me are you, my God, present on the altar, you, the Most Holy, the Creator of all peoples and the Lord of the angels. On such pilgrimages, travelers are often led by curiosity and love of novelty, and seldom do we hear that they come back with much spiritual gain. But here in the sacrament of the altar, you, my God, are wholly present, you, the fruit of eternal salvation, is bestowed, as often as you are worthily and devoutly received. It is not curiosity or levity or pleasure of the senses that draws us here, but firm faith and ardent hope and sincere love.

Prayers of Intercession

Adapted from the *Liturgy of the Word for Good Friday*

Let us pray.

Guide the course of events so that your Church may have the freedom to bring salvation to people everywhere. Lord, in your mercy, **hear our prayer**.

Grant our Holy Father, the Pope, good health and wisdom so that he may lead God's people. Lord, in your mercy, **hear our prayer**.

Assist our bishops, priests, and deacons to do your work more perfectly, to increase our faith, and to make us more discerning and more loving followers of Christ. Lord, in your mercy, **hear our prayer**.

Shepherd all those preparing for baptism, forgive their sins in the waters of new life, and grant them a new beginning in Jesus Christ, our Lord. Lord, in your mercy, **hear our prayer**.

Gather together in one Church all those who share our faith in Jesus Christ. Lord, in your mercy, **hear our prayer**.

Enlighten those who do not believe in Christ and show them the path to salvation through the grace of the Holy Spirit. Lord, in your mercy, **hear our prayer**.

Watch over all those in public office and inspire their hearts and minds so that peace and freedom may reign in this world. Lord, in your mercy, **hear our prayer**.

Give special attention to all those in need—the sick, the dying, the unjustly imprisoned, and rid the world of falsehood, hunger, poverty, and disease. Lord, in your mercy, **hear our prayer**.

We ask all this through Christ, our Lord. Amen.

Litany of Praise of the Most Precious Blood of Jesus

Lord, have mercy on us. Christ, **have mercy on us.**
Lord, have mercy on us. Christ, hear us. Christ, **graciously hear us.**
God, the Father of Heaven, **have mercy on us.**
God, the Son, Redeemer of the world, **have mercy on us.**
Holy Trinity, One God, **have mercy on us.**

Blood of Christ, Only Begotten Son of the Eternal Father, **save us.**
Blood of Christ, of the new and eternal testament, **save us.**

Blood of Christ, falling upon the earth in the agony, **save us.**

Blood of Christ, flowing forth in the crowning with thorns, **save us.**

Blood of Christ, poured out on the cross, **save us.**

Blood of Christ, price of our salvation, **save us.**

Blood of Christ, without which there is no forgiveness, **save us.**

Blood of Christ, refreshment of souls, **save us.**

Blood of Christ, river of mercy, **save us.**

Blood of Christ, victor over demons, **save us.**

Blood of Christ, courage of martyrs, **save us.**

Blood of Christ, strength of confessors, **save us.**

Blood of Christ, help of those in peril, **save us.**

Blood of Christ, relief of the burdened, **save us.**

Blood of Christ, solace in sorrow, **save us.**

Blood of Christ, hope of the penitent, **save us.**

Blood of Christ, consolation of the dying, **save us.**

Blood of Christ, peace and tenderness of hearts, **save us.**

Blood of Christ, pledge of eternal life, **save us.**

Blood of Christ, freeing souls from purgatory, **save us.**

Blood of Christ, most worthy of all glory and honor, **save us.**

Lamb of God, who takes away the sins of the world,
spare us, O Lord.

Lamb of God, who takes away the sins of the world,
graciously hear us, O Lord.

Lamb of God, who takes away the sins of the world,
have mercy on us.

Celebrant: Let us pray. Almighty and eternal God, you have appointed your Only Begotten Son the Redeemer of the world and willed to be appeased by his Blood. Grant, we ask of you, that we may worthily adore this price of our salvation, and through its power be safeguarded from the evils of this present life, so that we may rejoice in its fruits forever in heaven. Through the same Christ, our Lord. Amen.

Visits to the Blessed Sacrament and Our Lady

by St. Alphonsus Liguori

The following prayers and meditations come from the first "visit" of St. Alphonsus' popular *Visits to the Blessed Sacrament and Our Lady.*

Prayer Before Each Visit

My Lord Jesus Christ, because of your love for us, you remain night and day in the Blessed Sacrament, full of mercy and of love, waiting for, calling, and welcoming everyone who comes to visit you. I believe that you are present here on the altar. I adore you, and I thank you for all the graces you have bestowed on me; especially for having given me yourself in this sacrament, for having given me your most holy Mother, Mary, to plead for me, and for having called me to visit you in this church. I now speak to your most loving heart to thank you for this great gift and to make amends to you for all the insults given to you in this sacrament by your enemies, promising to adore you in all the places on earth in which you are present in the Blessed Sacrament and in which you are least honored and most abandoned.

My Jesus, I love you with my whole heart. I am very sorry for having refused your infinite goodness so many times. With the help of your grace, I resolve never to offend you again. Unworthy though I am, I now consecrate myself to you without reserve. I renounce my own will, my affections, my desires, and everything that I possess. I give them completely to you. All I ask of you is your holy love, final perseverance, and that I may carry out your will perfectly.

I commend to you the souls in purgatory, especially those who had the greatest devotion to the Blessed Sacrament and to the Blessed Virgin Mary. I also pray to you for all poor sinners. Finally, my dear Savior, I unite all my desires with the desires of your most loving heart. I offer them to the eternal Father and ask him, in your name and for love of you, to accept and grant them.

Visit to the Blessed Sacrament

Jesus in the Blessed Sacrament is the source of everything that is good. He says to us, "Let anyone who thirsts come to me and drink" (John 7:37). What graces the saints have drawn from the fountain of the Blessed Sacrament. It is there that Jesus distributes all the merits of his passion, as the prophet Isaiah foretold: "With joy you will draw water from the fountains of salvation" (Isaiah 12:3).

The Countess of Feria, who afterward became a Poor Clare nun, was called the spouse of the Blessed Sacrament because of her long and frequent visits. When she was asked how she spent the many hours passed in this way in the presence of the Holy of Holies, she replied, "I could remain there for eternity. The very essence of God, which will be the food of the blessed in heaven, is really present. And you ask me what I do in his presence? Why not ask me what I do not do there? I love him, I praise and thank him, and I appeal to him. What does a poor man do in the presence of a rich man? What does a sick person do in the presence of her doctor? What does a woman parched with thirst do when she comes to a clear fountain? What does a starving person do when he is sitting down for a delicious meal?"

My beloved Jesus, you who are my life, my hope, my treasure, and the only love of my heart, what has it cost you to remain with us in the Blessed Sacrament? You had to die a shameful death in order to dwell spiritually among us. Because you wanted to help us by your presence on our altars, how many insults have you not had to endure since then? Your love for us, and the desire you have that we should love you, have triumphed over everything.

Come then, Lord, come into my heart. Close its doors forever so that, in the future, no creature may enter it to share the love which is due to you, that love which I desire to give entirely to you. Let you alone, dear Redeemer, lead me; let you alone possess my whole being. If ever I do not obey you perfectly, correct me firmly that I may be more careful to please you in the future. Grant that I may never again seek any pleasure other than that of pleasing you, of visiting you often, of speaking with you, and of receiving you in holy Communion.

Let those who wish for them seek other treasures; I want to remember only your goodness. Blessed Seraphim, I envy you, not for your glory but for the love you have for our God. Teach me what I must do to love him and to please him.

Prayer of Spiritual Communion

My Jesus, I believe that you are present in the Blessed Sacrament. I love you above all things, and I desire to receive you into my soul. Since I am unable now to receive you sacramentally, come at least spiritually into my heart. I embrace you as being already there and unite myself wholly to you; do not permit me to be ever separated from you.

Visit to Our Lady

Our Mother Mary is another fountain from which we can also draw the waters of grace. Saint Bernard says that she is so rich in graces that there is no one in the world who does not benefit from them. The angel greeted her with the words, "Hail! Full of grace!" The Blessed Virgin was filled with grace by God that she might afterward give it to all who are devoted to her.

Prayer to Our Lady

Most holy Virgin Immaculate, my Mother, Mary, you are the Mother of my Lord, the Queen of the world, the advocate, the hope, and the refuge of sinners. I, who am most in need of mercy, come before you today. I offer you my respectful devotion, and I thank you for all the graces you have granted to me until now. In particular, I thank you for saving me from hell, which I have so often deserved by my sins. I love you, most lovable Lady. Because of my love for you, I promise to honor you always and to do all in my power to make sure that others also love you. In your hands I place all my hopes; I entrust the saving of my soul to your care. Accept me as your servant, Mother of Mercy; take me under your mantle. Because you have such power with God, save me always from temptations, or rather, obtain for me, until my death, the strength to overcome them. Of you I ask the grace of a perfect love for Jesus Christ. With your help, I hope to die a happy death. My Mother, I beg you, by the love you have for God, to help me at all times, but especially at the last moment of my life. Do not leave me, I plead with you, until you see me safe in heaven, blessing you and singing your mercy for eternity. Amen.

That is my hope. May it be so.

Section Four

Praying With the Psalms

PRAYER IN THE MORNING

O God, come to my assistance.

—O Lord, make haste to help me.

Glory to the Father, and to the Son, and to the Holy Spirit:

—As it was in the beginning, is now, and will be forever. Amen. (Alleluia.)

Morning Hymn

From *"All That Dwell Below the Skies,"* Isaac Watts (1674–1748)

From all that dwell below the skies,
Let the Creator's praise arise;
Let the Redeemer's name be sung,
Through ev'ry land by ev'ry tongue.

Eternal are thy mercies, Lord;
Eternal truth attends thy word:
Thy praise shall sound from shore to shore,
Till suns shall rise and set no more.

(OR)

Morning Hymn

"Morning Has Broken," Eleanor Farjeon (1931)

Morning has broken
like the first morning,
blackbird has spoken
like the first bird.
Praise for the singing!
Praise for the morning!
Praise for them, springing
fresh from the Word!

Sweet the rain's new fall
sunlit from heaven,
like the first dewfall
on the first grass.
Praise for the sweetness
of the wet garden,
sprung in completeness
where God's feet pass.

Mine is the sunlight!
Mine is the morning
born of the one light
Eden saw play!
Praise with elation,
praise every morning,
God's recreation
of the new day!

Psalm 63:2–9

Antiphon: ***My soul is thirsting for you, O Lord my God.***

O God, you are my God—
it is you I seek!
For you my body yearns;
for you my soul thirsts,
In a land parched, lifeless,
and without water.

I look to you in the sanctuary
to see your power and glory.
For your love is better than life;
my lips shall ever praise you!

I will bless you as long as I live;
I will lift up my hands, calling on your name.
My soul shall be sated as with choice food,
with joyous lips my mouth shall praise you!

I think of you upon my bed,
I remember you through the watches of the night.
You indeed are my savior,
and in the shadow of your wings I shout for joy.
My soul clings fast to you;
your right hand upholds me.

Antiphon: ***My soul is thirsting for you, O Lord my God.***

Psalm 138

Antiphon: ***In the presence of the angels, I will give you thanks, O Lord.***

I thank you, Lord, with all my heart;
in the presence of the angels to you I sing.
I bow low toward your holy temple;
I praise your name for your mercy and faithfulness.

For you have exalted over all
your name and your promise.
On the day I cried out, you answered;
you strengthened my spirit.

All the kings of earth will praise you, LORD,
when they hear the words of your mouth.
They will sing of the ways of the LORD,
"How great is the glory of the LORD!"

The LORD is on high, but cares for the lowly
and knows the proud from afar.
Though I walk in the midst of dangers,
you guard my life when my enemies rage.

You stretch out your hand;
your right hand saves me.
The LORD is with me to the end.
LORD, your mercy endures forever.
Never forsake the work of your hands!

Antiphon: ***In the presence of the angels, I will give you thanks, O Lord.***

Reading: **Luke 9:11–17**

The crowds...followed [Jesus]. He received them and spoke to them about the kingdom of God, and he healed those who needed to be cured. As the day was drawing to a close, the Twelve approached him and said, "Dismiss the crowd so that they can go to the surrounding villages and farms and find lodging and provisions; for we are in a deserted place here." He said to them, "Give them some food yourselves." They replied, "Five loaves and two fishes are all we have, unless we ourselves go and buy food for all these people." Now the men there numbered about five thousand. Then he said to his disciples, "Have them sit down in groups of [about] fifty." They did so and made them all sit down. Then taking the five loaves and the two fish, and looking up to heaven, he said the blessing over them, broke them, and gave them to the disciples to set before the crowd. They all ate and were satisfied. And when the leftover fragments were picked up, they filled twelve wicker baskets.

Responsory

The Lord has given us food, bread of the finest wheat,
—The Lord has given us food, bread of the finest wheat.
Honey from the rock to our heart's content,
—bread of the finest wheat.
Glory to the Father, and to the Son, and to the Holy Spirit.
—The Lord has given us food, bread of the finest wheat.

Canticle of Zechariah

Blessed be the Lord, the God of Israel;
he has come to his people and set them free.

He has raised up for us a mighty savior,
born of the house of his servant David.

Through his holy prophets he promised of old
that he would save us from our enemies,
from the hands of all who hate us.
He promised to show mercy to our fathers
and to remember his holy covenant.

This was the oath he swore to our father Abraham:
to set us free from the hands of our enemies,

free to worship him without fear,
holy and righteous in his sight all the days of our life.

You, my child, shall be called the prophet of the Most High;
for you will go before the Lord to prepare his way,
to give his people knowledge of salvation
by the forgiveness of their sins.

In the tender compassion of our God
the dawn from on high shall break upon us,
to shine on those who dwell in darkness and the shadow of death,
and to guide our feet into the way of peace.

Intercessions

Christ is the Bread of Life and the Cup of our Salvation. Let us call out to him in praise:

For the Church: for bishops and pastors, teachers and catechists, confessors and spiritual directors, and for all believers, ***Lord in your mercy...Hear our prayer.***

For peace: for an end to war among the nations and strife within families and communities, ***Lord in your mercy...Hear our prayer.***

For the suffering: for those who are infirmed, those who live with chronic pain, those who are lonely, and all who are in harm's way, ***Lord in your mercy...Hear our prayer.***

For the faithful departed: for those who have died... *(names).* And for those who mourn, ***Lord in your mercy...Hear our prayer.***

For all who need our prayer: for those for whom we are concerned...*(pause for silent prayer).* For those for whom we have promised to pray, ***Lord in your mercy...Hear our prayer.***

The Lord's Prayer

We pray as Jesus taught us:

Our Father, who art in heaven,
hallowed be thy name;
thy kingdom come;
thy will be done on earth as it is in heaven.
Give us this day our daily bread,
and forgive us our trespasses
as we forgive those who trespass against us;
and lead us not into temptation,
but deliver us from evil.

Concluding Prayer

Gracious God,
true light and source of all light,
listen to our morning prayer.
Turn our thoughts to what is holy
that we may ever live in the light of your love.
We ask this through our Lord Jesus Christ, your Son,
who lives and reigns with you
and the Holy Spirit, one God, for ever and ever.
Amen.

Dismissal

May the Lord bless us,
protect us from all evil, and bring us to everlasting life.
Amen.

Prayer in the Evening

O God, come to my assistance.
—O Lord, make haste to help me.
Glory to the Father, and to the Son, and to the Holy Spirit:
—As it was in the beginning, is now, and will be forever.
Amen. (Alleluia.)

Hymn

"Now Thank We All Our God," Martin Rinkart (c.1636); translated by Catherine Winkworth (1856)

Now thank we all our God,
With heart and hands and voices,
Who wondrous things has done,
In whom his world rejoices;
Who from our mothers' arms
Has blessed us on our way
With countless gifts of love,
And still is ours today.

O may this gracious God
Through all our life be near us,
With ever joyful hearts.
And blessed peace to cheer us;
Preserve us in his grace,
And guide us in distress,
And free us from all sin,
Till heaven we possess.

All praise and thanks to God
The Father now be given,
The Son and Spirit blest,
Who reigns in highest heaven;
Eternal, Triune God,
Whom earth and heaven adore;
For thus it was, is now,
And shall be ever more.

(OR)

Hymn

"Lord, Who at Thy First Eucharist Didst Pray," W. H. Turton (1881)

Lord, who at thy first Eucharist didst pray,
That all thy Church might be forever one,
Grant us at every Eucharist to say
With longing heart and soul, "Thy will be done."
Oh, may we all one bread, one body be,
Through this blest sacrament of unity.

For all thy Church, O Lord, we intercede;
Make thou our sad divisions soon to cease;
Draw us the nearer each to each, we plead,
By drawing all to thee, O prince of peace;
Thus may we all one bread, one body be,
Through this blest sacrament of unity.

We pray thee, too, for wanderers from thy fold,
Oh, bring them back, good shepherd of the sheep,
Back to the faith which saints believed of old,
Back to the Church which still that faith doth keep;
Soon may we all one bread, one body be,
Through this blest sacrament of unity.

So, Lord, at length when sacraments shall cease,
May we be one with all thy Church above,
One with thy saints in one unbroken peace,
One with thy saints in one unbounded love;
More blessed still, in peace and love to be
One with the trinity in unity.

Psalm 42:4–6

Antiphon: ***Let us celebrate with joy in the presence of our Lord and King.***

As the deer longs
for streams of water,
so my soul longs
for you, O God.

My soul thirsts for God,
the living God.
When can I enter and see
the face of God?

My tears have been my bread
day and night,
as they ask me every day,
"Where is your God?"

Those times I recall
as I pour out my soul,
When I would cross over to
the shrine of the Mighty One,
to the house of God,
Amid loud cries of thanksgiving,
with the multitude keeping festival.

Why are you downcast, my soul;
why do you groan within me?
Wait for God, for I shall again praise him,
my savior and my God.

Antiphon: ***Let us celebrate with joy in the presence of our Lord and King.***

Psalm 34:2–11

Antiphon: ***Taste and see the goodness of the Lord.***

I will bless the LORD at all times;
his praise shall be always in my mouth.
My soul will glory in the LORD;
let the poor hear and be glad.

Magnify the LORD with me;
and let us exalt his name together.
I sought the LORD, and he answered me,
delivered me from all my fears.

Look to him and be radiant,
and your faces may not blush for shame.
This poor one cried out and the LORD heard,
and from all his distress he saved him.

The angel of the LORD encamps
around those who fear him, and he saves them.
Taste and see that the LORD is good;
blessed is the stalwart one who takes refuge in him.

Fear the LORD, you his holy ones;
nothing is lacking to those who fear him.
The rich grow poor and go hungry,
but those who seek the LORD lack no good thing.

Antiphon: ***Taste and see the goodness of the Lord.***

Reading

Romans 12:9–12

Let love be sincere; hate what is evil, hold on to what is good; love one another with mutual affection; anticipate one another in showing honor. Do not grow slack in zeal, be fervent in spirit, serve the Lord. Rejoice in hope, endure in affliction, persevere in prayer.

Responsory

We give thanks to you, O God, as we call upon your name.
—We give thanks to you, O God, as we call upon your name.
We marvel at your merciful love for us,
—as we call upon your name.
Glory to the Father, and to the Son, and to the Holy Spirit.
—We give thanks to you, O God, as we call upon your name.

***Meditation:* From *Dominicae Cenae*—Pope Saint John Paul II**

The Eucharist...shows us...what value each person, our brother or sister, has in God's eyes, if Christ offers himself equally to each one, under the species of bread and wine. If our Eucharistic worship is authentic, it must make us grow in awareness of the dignity of each person.... Christ comes into the hearts of our brothers and sisters and visits their consciences. How the image of each and every one changes, when we become aware of this reality, when we make it the subject of our reflections!

Canticle of Mary

My soul proclaims the greatness of the Lord,
my spirit rejoices in God my Savior
for he has looked with favor on his lowly servant.

From this day all generations will call me blessed:
the Almighty has done great things for me,
and holy is his name.

He has mercy on those who fear him
in every generation.

He has shown the strength of his arm,
he has scattered the proud in their conceit.
He has cast down the mighty from their thrones,

and has lifted up the lowly.
He has filled the hungry with good things,
and the rich he has sent away empty.

He has come to the help of his servant Israel
for he has remembered his promise of mercy,
the promise he made to our fathers,
to Abraham and his children for ever.

Intercessions

Confident in your power to provide what we need, we pray:

For the Church: for bishops and pastors and all who are responsible for the care of souls, we pray... **Lord, hear our prayer.**

For the leaders of nations and all who are responsible for keeping the peace, protecting the vulnerable, and ensuring access to the necessities of life for every person, we pray... **Lord, hear our prayer.**

For the sick, the suffering, and all those who most need our prayers, we pray... **Lord, hear our prayer.**

For those who have died and those who mourn, we pray... **Lord, hear our prayer.**

For our needs and intentions *(pause for prayer)*. With faith in your power to provide what we need, we pray... **Lord, hear our prayer.**

The Lord's Prayer

We pray as Jesus taught us:

Our Father, who art in heaven,
hallowed be thy name;
thy kingdom come;
thy will be done on earth as it is in heaven.
Give us this day our daily bread,
and forgive us our trespasses
as we forgive those who trespass against us;
and lead us not into temptation,
but deliver us from evil.

Concluding Prayer

God our Father,
you have filled the hungry with the good things of heaven.
Keep in mind your infinite compassion.
Look upon our poverty,
and let us share the riches of your life and love.
We ask this through our Lord Jesus Christ, your Son,
who lives and reigns with you and the Holy Spirit,
one God, for ever and ever.
Amen.

Dismissal

May the Lord bless us,
protect us from all evil and bring us to everlasting life.
Amen.

Meditation from Pope John Paul II: In My Own Words,
compiled by Anthony F. Chiffolo, Liguori Publications (813771)

Section Five

Suggestions for a Private Visit to the Blessed Sacrament

Time spent reflecting in the presence of Jesus Christ is time gratefully accepted from the Lord, who graces us here on earth with his loving presence. It is time that merits for us eternal life. People who think they are too busy to pray should listen to the call:

"Awake, O sleeper,
and arise from the dead,
and Christ will give you light" (Ephesians 5:14).

If we become aware of Christ's presence, he will alert our senses to fuller life and make us, through him, light for the world. From this short exposure to Christ in our visits to the Blessed Sacrament, there arises a sharper awareness of the preciousness of time: "[Make] the most of the opportunity, because the days are evil" (Ephesians 5:16).

Once, a priest asked a young man what he did during all the hours he spent before the tabernacle. The response was simple: "I let my soul enjoy the sunshine!"

To better utilize this time in God's presence, the following suggestions can be useful:

1. Adore God.

The burning lamp near the tabernacle invites us to remember the gracious nearness of Jesus, who came like a candle to bring warmth, peace, and light into the world, and spent himself finally on the cross to enter into the fullness of the Father's glory.

Before the tabernacle, we adore the eternal Word who took flesh and became one of us to enlighten everyone. In adoration, our faith in the Paschal Mystery lifts our hearts, and we meditate on the words from the Book of Revelation: "At once I was caught up in spirit. A throne was there in heaven, and on the throne sat one whose appearance sparkled like jasper and carnelian. Around the throne was a halo as brilliant as an emerald.... Then I saw standing in the midst of the throne and the four living creatures and the elders a Lamb that seemed to have been slain" (Revelation 4:2–3; 5:6). Turning our eyes and hearts to this Lamb, we say with Thomas, "My Lord and my God!"

The Lamb standing before the Father's throne is the eternal intercessor. The Father remembers forever that his Son, who became man, bears this slaughter for us, thus calling to mind his "holy covenant" (Luke 1:72).

Silent adoration before the tabernacle is a wholesome remembrance, a training for a healthy, grateful memory that brings us closer to the Faithful One who remembers us by his gracious presence in our midst.

To make our time of remembrance before the tabernacle or monstrance more fruitful, here are two suggestions. One is to meditate from time to time on the official eucharistic prayers of the Mass, word by word. By letting the words enter deeply into our hearts, we will experience the depth and wealth of these texts with greater joy during our next participation in the Mass.

The second suggestion is that we meditate on all the great mysteries of creation: the Incarnation of the Word of God; the passion, death, resurrection, and ascension of Jesus Christ into heaven; and the descent of the Holy Spirit on his Church. Thus reminded, we can examine our own lives and give thanks for the countless blessings we have received. Don't leave out the disappointments, sufferings, or daily crosses; try to fit them into the whole picture as they blend with the Lamb marked by the signs of slaughter. We can then praise the Lord, who, through his death, resurrection, and eucharistic union with us, has given our wounds a new meaning.

As we sit or kneel before the tabernacle, we should be ever thankful that our joys and sufferings, which for unbelievers can prove frustrating, make sense to us and lead us to share in the history of salvation because we are living in profound union with the Holy Redeemer.

2. *Pray "Lord, Here I Am!"*

Before the self-giving presence of our Lord in the Blessed Sacrament, we remember the many times when he nourished our faith, hope, and love with his Body and Blood. By giving himself to us, he encourages us to give ourselves to him. Our reflective adoration before the Blessed Sacrament becomes a prayer of readiness: "Lord, here I am! Accept me! Transform me! Send me!" We can begin to examine the critical areas of our daily life: our relationships with our neighbors, with those who misunderstand us, with those who oppose us, with those who need greater love and affirmation from us, and with those who need our healing and reconciling love.

In his letter *On the Mystery and Worship of the Eucharist,* Pope St. John Paul II writes, "This veneration [of the Eucharist] arises from love and fosters the love to which we are called." Let us, then, constantly pray to the Lamb marked with the signs of slaughter for the same kind of love that he has shown us. He died for us sinners; he offered himself up for us who, by our sins, have rebelled against him. On the cross, he cried out to the Father for us, "Father, forgive them, they know not what they do" (Luke 23:34).

By creating a new life within us at holy Communion, Jesus calls us to imitate his kind of love. In this light, we take a new look at our relationships with those who have hurt us or those whom we have hurt. We pray to Jesus to conform our hearts to his, to strengthen us with a healing, reconciling love. We should also pray frequently before the tabernacle: "Have mercy on us, O Lord, for we have sinned against you," and thus open ourselves to the charism of healing love that will wipe out all hatred.

As we bring our personal experiences, our individual needs, and all our hurts to our Lord in the Blessed Sacrament, we cannot forget that the object of our adoration is the "Lamb of God who takes upon himself the burden of the sin of the world;" the Peacemaker who prevails over violence. In his presence, our prayer—"Lord, here I am!"—becomes our mission and readiness to make our best contributions for a peaceful world; a system of nonviolence everywhere and on all levels.

3. *Try to Understand God's Will for You.*

We spend our time well before the tabernacle in silent prayer, meditation, and thanksgiving when, in the presence of our Lord, we try to discern what the will of God is for us. We know that we can do nothing for salvation by ourselves. Therefore, we should listen to the exhortation of the apostle: "Be filled with the Spirit" (Ephesians 5:18).

When we gratefully allow our Lord to shine upon us and illumine us by the mysteries on which we meditate and glorify in this sacrament, we can be assured that the Holy Spirit will permeate us, guide us, and strengthen us. Our willing attitude puts us on the same wavelength as the Holy Spirit, who will help us examine our desires, refine our plans, and analyze our capabilities so that we can sincerely offer them to Jesus as signs of our ardent gratitude. It is then that we begin to see clearly what we must renounce and what we need to cultivate in ourselves, our surroundings, and our lifestyles.

4. *Pray "Come, Lord Jesus!"*

We have seen that the sacramental presence of Christ in the Eucharist is the Paschal Mystery reaching out to us. It is the Paschal Mystery made present by the coming of Jesus, who is the glory of the Father. Our eucharistic veneration would be neither sound nor healing if we were to neglect this dimension. We look forward to the final coming of the Lord: "The Spirit and the bride say, 'Come.' Let the hearer say 'Come.' Let the one who thirsts come forward, and the one who wants it receive the gift of life-giving water" (Revelation 22:17).

A genuine eucharistic devotion causes us to long for the final coming of the Lord, to long for our homecoming, and to long for all creation to live with the ultimate freedom as children of our Father. God is infinitely generous and rich in his gifts, but the gift of freedom will be given only to those who desire it. Eucharistic worship helps us free ourselves from useless desires and cares, opening us to the living water that wells up for eternal life.

Our willingness to pray "Lord, here I am!" and our effort to discern, in the presence of the Lord, what the will of God is, prepare us for our mission, our responsibility in the world. The more we listen to him who says, "Yes, I am coming soon," the more our manner of life responds, "Amen! Come, Lord Jesus!" (Revelation 22:20).

5. *Submit to Him with the Words "Your Kingdom Come."*

Although we emphasize the importance of eucharistic devotion here, we do so with no intention of "privatizing" religion. When we say "Come!" with the Spirit, we also pray, with all our hearts, "Your kingdom come." Through eucharistic veneration, we enter more deeply into the dimensions of the kingdom of God, a kingdom of love, peace, and justice.

In silent contemplation and adoration before the Blessed Sacrament, we open ourselves to his liberating love, his saving justice, and his forgiving mission. We say to our Lord, “Here I am! Send me!” With a heart earnestly craving that the kingdom of God may reach all people, we pray that God’s will be done. Letting our devotion shine before the world, we can hope that our actions will turn people’s attention to the Lord when they see the good we do. (See Matthew 5:16.)

Section Six

A Brief History of the Forty Hours Devotion

Christian liturgy is an ever-evolving set of movements, texts, and roles, and the Forty Hours devotion combines elements of ancient practice with creative, novel rituals that support the effort to praise God in the holy Eucharist. Even from the first moments of Jesus' life, when the Magi and shepherds were present, we glimpse hints of the importance of placing our mind and gaze in adoration to the Divine Majesty.

The scriptural significance of the number forty is apparent in the Old and New Testaments: the Israelites roamed the desert for forty years, and Jesus fasted for forty days in the desert prior to engaging in his public ministry. Tradition holds that forty also reflects the number of hours from the time of Christ's death to his resurrection.

The Forty Hours devotion has a rich history steeped in the development and practice of perpetual adoration. Medieval monasteries occasionally conducted perpetual adoration (*laus perennis*), a continuous recitation of the Divine Office, day and night, without interruption. In 1226, perpetual adoration of the Blessed Sacrament was introduced in Avignon, France, by King Louis VIII and continued until the French Revolution. Corpus Christi rites soon introduced a procession and Benediction with the Body of Christ to the practice. Some religious communities built their charisms around the Eucharist as well. In 1695, Mother Mechtilde (Catherine de Bar), a French Benedictine nun, founded an order of sisters dedicated solely to perpetual adoration of the Blessed Sacrament. The Forty Hours devotion became an amalgamation of these rites.

Some scholars mark the formal beginning of the Forty Hours devotion in 1527, when St. Anthony Mary Zaccaria, founder of the Barnabites, instituted the devotion in Milan. Others point to Joseph Piantanida da Fermo, a Capuchin friar, as the person who arranged to have the devotion move between churches. Milan's Church of the Holy Sepulchre (San Sepolcro), whose very name suggests the importance of prayer over forty hours, became a locus for the rite, and a confraternity grew up around it. Soon, an indulgence was attached to the practice. Granted by Pope Paul III in 1539 "to appease the anger of God," the prayers of successive churches over forty hours were seen as worthy of promotion.

Later popes followed suit, even mandating that the Forty Hours devotion be performed throughout Rome; the devotion had arrived in the city thanks to St. Philip Neri. In his 1592 decree, *Graves et diuturnae*, Pope Clement VIII sought to make Rome's participation such that "at every hour of the day and night, the whole year round, the incense of prayer shall ascend without intermission before the face of the Lord."

Not only have Church authorities sought to influence the spread of the devotion, but eucharistic exposition has occasionally led to miraculous phenomena. One such instance occurred in 1608 at a Benedictine monastery in Faverney, France. On the night before Pentecost, the monks decided to erect a temporary altar for eucharistic adoration and, placing a monstrance with two hosts in the lunette upon the altar, sung Vespers and left the Blessed Sacrament in place. The following day, the monks opened the church to find the altar reduced to ashes by fire, but the monstrance with the hosts remained suspended in midair, unharmed by the blaze. A new altar was erected, and the monstrance came to rest upon it. Today, it is possible to venerate the eucharistic hosts that survived the fire.

Spiritual anomalies such as the one in France may have prompted greater circumspection. Guidelines for the Forty Hours devotion were formalized by Pope Clement XII in the document *Instructio Clementina* in 1736. Thirty-seven specific rules were issued, instructing Rome's churches—except the major basilicas—to give homage to the exposed Eucharist in the Forty Hours. Guidelines were established for the prayers, hymns, processions, and other liturgical acts associated with the devotion. With some modifications, these rules have formed the basis for modern, diocese-wide performance of the Forty Hours.

St. John Neumann, CSsR
Forty Hours Devotion in the United States

When he became bishop of Philadelphia in 1852, St. John Neumann was already acquainted with the variety of Catholic cultures in his vast diocese. Neither language nor economic status could unite the differing cultures. However, they shared a common religious experience: the Eucharist. While serving as a Redemptorist missionary in Pennsylvania and Maryland before his assignment as bishop, John Neumann had ample opportunity to understand how a visible eucharistic practice could invite retribution, with detractors hurling epithets or worse at him. When he became bishop, some cautioned him against public displays, such as processions.

Bishop Neumann looked to his past for an answer to overcoming the many cultural differences and anti-Catholic sentiments in his diocese. As a boy, he was attuned to ritual; his home in Prachatice, in Bohemia (today's Czech Republic), was very close to the village church. As a seminarian in Budweis, Neumann would have known about the legacy of the diocese's first bishop, Johann Prokop Schaffgotsch (bishop from 1785–1813), who began a Forty Hours devotion in 1799 to implore God's protection from the perils of war then raging in the land. By the time Neumann arrived for studies in 1823, the devotion was an established tradition in the diocesan Cathedral of St. Nicholas.

The story of Bishop Neumann's commission of the Forty Hours devotion comes to us from his confessor. One night, the Bishop awoke to find a candle overturned on his desk, burning his papers, and he managed to extinguish it quickly. The papers had been only slightly charred. At that moment, he heard a voice telling him, "Go on and order the Forty Hours devotion! My sacrament is a light that shines and warms everywhere, no matter where it is placed, and just as you see this candle burn without the paper burning...so my sacrament, though in the midst of profanation, has a power in itself which will keep it from contamination."

Confronted with hostilities from Protestant Nativists in his sprawling diocese, Bishop Neumann sought a familiar mechanism to bind his people together and implore God's protective help. He introduced the prospect of a Forty Hours devotion at a diocesan synod in April 1853, then commenced the devotion the following month. In his plan, Bishop Neumann decreed to all diocesan clergy that there would be an annual cycle of constant prayer in parishes and mission chapels scattered throughout Pennsylvania, New Jersey, and Delaware. He launched the initial devotion from the parish of St. Philip Neri in Philadelphia. This church was probably selected because it played an important role in the anti-Catholic riots of 1844, and perhaps to honor the saint who had spread the devotion in Rome. Bishop Neumann preached at the opening Mass, and reports speak of an enormous crowd.

In the first year of the devotion, about a dozen parishes participated. The following year, the number quadrupled. Bishop Neumann is therefore credited with establishing the Forty Hours devotion in the United States. Seeing the popularity and potential of the devotion, the Bishop immediately wrote to the Congregation for the Propagation of the Faith to obtain a plenary indulgence for his diocese. After consultation with Pope Pius IX, it was granted on July 22, 1855. In that year, Bishop Neumann developed a manual for clergy pertaining to the conduct of the devotion.

The devotion had the benefit of giving people an opportunity, day and night, to pour out their prayers to Jesus and extol his mercy for their needs. By 1856, the diocesan-wide salute to the Divine Majesty was firmly in place, and a calendar was issued in English at the end of every year to inform the faithful where the devotion would be conducted on any given week.

Bishop Neumann's fellow bishops also issued instructions on the incorporation of the Forty Hours devotion into their dioceses. Just months after Bishop Neumann began the devotion, Bishop John Timon of Buffalo followed his example. In Baltimore, Archbishop Francis Kenrick also encouraged his clergy to promote the devotion.

Because of Bishop Neumann's innovation, in 1866, the Second Plenary Council of Baltimore established definite parameters for the conduct of the Forty Hours, including the limitation of exposition to daylight hours only, along with the omission of a procession at the discretion of the pastor. All parish members who could do so were encouraged to make a brief visit to the church while the Eucharist was exposed.

It should be noted that St. John Neumann was not the first to celebrate the Forty Hours or nocturnal adoration in the United States. One isolated example occurred in 1845, where Fr. Francis Brunner, CPPS, wrote to Bishop John Baptist Purcell of Cincinnati, stating that several of the Sisters of the Precious Blood were commencing overnight adoration. Fr. Brunner asked for permission to have the Forty Hours available for the sisters.

Redemptorists and the Forty Hours

Generations of Redemptorists have cultivated a sincere attachment to the Eucharist. From the time of their novitiate to their golden years, Redemptorists make a Holy Hour, helping to cultivate a special reverence for the Eucharist. It is not unusual to walk into house chapels and find them praying before a monstrance.

This prompting was inspired by the founder of the Redemptorist Congregation, St. Alphonsus Liguori, whose own love for the Eucharist is well known. In his *Visits to the Blessed Sacrament and Our Lady,* he speaks of a spiritual communion with Jesus. He wrote the book "with the sole purpose of strengthening people more and more with the love of Jesus Christ." In this book, St. Alphonsus references many saints who showed companionship with our Lord in the Blessed Sacrament by visiting him frequently with true devotion and love.

The Redemptorists record many examples of how the Forty Hours devotion has been fostered. An early instance is from New Orleans. Already an annual practice of the St. Alphonsus parish—St. Mary's Assumption Church, St. Alphonsus Church, and Notre Dame de Bon Secours—on March 6, 1858, St. Mary's Assumption Church received a silver-gilt monstrance from France explicitly for the devotion. The Redemptorist house chronicler noted that the Forty Hours was a kind of antidote to the debaucheries of Mardi Gras that were occurring. "During these three days of the carnival, we had the Forty Hours Adoration in all the churches. The churches were well attended during the time, the confessionals were surrounded, and great numbers approached the sacrament, among whom were many who had neglected the sacraments for years."

For generations, Redemptorist prayer books have supplied numerous examples of how to pray before the Blessed Sacrament. For instance, in a 1934 edition of the booklet *Eucharistic Holy Hour,* Fr.

Joseph Picton, CSsR, noted that time with Jesus in the Eucharist is "a noble and sublime office of keeping the Divine Lord company in his bitter agony" in the Garden of Olives "to console and comfort his afflicted Heart." In *Parish Hymns and Devotions,* compiled by Fr. John M. Beierschmidt, CSsR, readers are urged to make a spiritual communion with the following words, taken from an Alphonsian prayer: "I embrace you as if you were already there, and unite myself wholly to you: never permit me to be separated from you."

The Redemptorists were often called upon to preach the Forty Hours devotion. In 1930, Redemptorists from Pittsburgh traveled to seven parishes in Pennsylvania and New York to conduct the Forty Hours. Redemptorists in St. Louis also preached to eleven parishes in 1940. One can also find references to the Redemptorist presence in small communities in Nebraska, Montana, Idaho, and California. Whether in metropolitan areas like Chicago or Los Angeles, Baltimore or San Antonio, they drew the faithful to the mercy and grace of the Eucharist.

In the 1960s, in the midst of the Second Vatican Council, an American priest wrote to Redemptorist Fr. Francis Connell, dean of Catholic moral theologians and professor at the Catholic University of America. The priest asked whether, because of low attendance, he could forego the Forty Hours as an annual practice. Fr. Connell replied, saying that because the pastor was under obligation to his bishop, who had instituted the devotion in the diocese, the pastor ought to continue holding the devotion. Fr. Connell also plainly stated that the pastor should consider that the Lord's invitation to his parishioners was ongoing. Exposition of the Blessed Sacrament meant that "our Lord is waiting, ready to bestow his graces on those who visit him."

At a Forty Hours celebration, another Redemptorist, Fr. John Reuf, CSsR, called the congregation to consider this sacrament of love. "Love detests separation," he said. The first thing that needs to be done at the time of the Forty Hours "is to renew our belief that Jesus is really present here in the Blessed Sacrament." Finally, when we receive his sacred Body in the sacrament of the Eucharist, he advised, "Thank him for staying with us from day to day and year to year." Similar words have been repeated on innumerable occasions, all emphasizing how vital keeping company with our Savior can be. The Forty Hours devotion gives us ample opportunity to do so.

Patrick Hayes, PhD
Redemptorist Archivist

Section Seven

Fostering Eucharistic Devotions

The core of eucharistic piety is frequent remembrance of past, present, and future celebrations of the Mass and its meaning for our lives, concerns, endeavors, and relationships. We express this devotion in an ideal way when, before Mass, we prepare our minds and hearts for the celebration. After Mass, we reflect on how, during that day or the rest of the week, we can foster and express abiding gratitude evoked by the eucharistic memorial.

Those who attend Sunday Mass and subsequently forget about what they have celebrated and received act irresponsibly. The main purpose of our eucharistic worship is to establish a growing relationship between receiving and giving, contemplation and action, divine rites and human rights, reverence for the mystery of holiness and familiarity with Jesus. Only by actively participating in this relationship will we overcome the gap between religion and our daily lives.

Two Vatican documents encourage such eucharistic piety: Instruction on Eucharistic Worship (*Eucharisticum Mysterium*), issued in 1967, and Pope St. John Paul II's letter *On the Mystery and Worship of the Eucharist,* issued in 1980. Both documents address appropriate and encouraged forms of eucharistic piety: celebration of the feast of Corpus Christi and its solemn procession, eucharistic congresses, periods of exposition of the Blessed Sacrament with solemn Benediction, annual celebration of the Forty Hours devotion, other hours of adoration, perpetual adoration in dioceses, and, last but not least, silent prayer before the tabernacle.

Throughout these suggested ways to foster a eucharistic spirituality, one never loses sight of the center and summit of Christian life: the celebration of the Mass with reception of holy Communion. The following sections present a brief history on some of the aforementioned forms of eucharistic piety.

Corpus Christi

Around 1209, a group of holy women in Liège, Belgium, established a center dedicated to eucharistic piety. These women were convinced that the Lord desired the celebration of a new feast dedicated to the reserved sacrament of the altar. This feast became known as Corpus Christi. For this feast, St. Thomas Aquinas composed beautiful hymns that expertly combined dogma with devotion.

With its rich eucharistic liturgy and procession, the feast of Corpus Christi is an occasion of special praise and thanksgiving offered to the Father in the name of all creation and of special thanksgiving for the institution of the Eucharist in which Christ's Body is the bread of life. It is an extension of the praise expressed in its very institution: "The Lord Jesus, on the night he was handed over, took bread and, after he had given thanks, broke it and said, 'This is my Body that is for you. Do this in remembrance of me.' In the same way also the cup, after supper, saying, 'This cup is the new covenant in my Blood. Do this, as often as you drink it, in remembrance of me.' For as often as you eat this bread and drink the cup, you proclaim the death of the Lord until he comes" (1 Corinthians 11:23–26).

Saint Augustine taught that eternal life is essentially praise and thanksgiving, and, therefore, a life lived in grateful praise is the road to final fulfillment. The feast of Corpus Christi was and is, in many parts of the Catholic Church, an occasion for creative forms of praise and thanksgiving.

The Corpus Christi procession is a solemn act of public adoration and praise; it is in perfect harmony with the eucharistic memorial. In many Catholic towns, the houses are decorated for this procession. There are beautiful arrangements of flowers, especially before the four altars where the gospels are chanted and solemn Benediction given. Church choirs and musicians also perform. Members of various associations, wearing their distinctive garb, add vivid color to the occasion. All this activity is done freely and generously, pointing to the praise for the Creator. The Corpus Christi procession is a kind of cosmic liturgy. Symbolically, it invites all creatures to join in the Church's joy, gratitude, and praise. Thus, festivity and solemnity combine in this eucharistic celebration and procession.

Solemn Benediction is another feature of the procession. At each altar, after the singing of the gospel and special prayers calling for the Lord's blessing on the four corners of the earth, there is a solemn blessing with the Blessed Sacrament in the monstrance. The prayer of praise and thanksgiving is itself a blessing from God, opening our hearts for renewed graces. Ordinarily, when we bless others on various occasions, we invoke almighty God. At the solemn eucharistic Benediction, it is evident that Christ himself blesses us and intends to make all of us a blessing for one another.

Church processions, but particularly the Corpus Christi procession, symbolize our pilgrimage on the road to our final destination, with Christ accompanying us, for he is the Way and our final home. The solemnity of the Most Holy Body and Blood of Christ (Corpus Christi) is a major feast in the Church today and is reverently celebrated on either Thursday or Sunday after Trinity Sunday by Catholic communities throughout the world.

Eucharistic Congresses

Eucharistic congresses on the national and international levels may be compared to celebrations of the feast of Corpus Christi on an enlarged scale. Drawing large crowds, they serve as powerful inspiration for the restoration of eucharistic veneration and—especially during the last decades—for the renewal of all who participate. The latest national and international eucharistic congresses have exemplified how traditional forms of eucharistic devotion can be easily adapted to new times, without any detriment to their former popular appeal. Although the first eucharistic congresses met with vehement opposition from Protestant churches, the more recent congresses have attracted an ecumenical audience due, in part, to an increased openness among all Christians.

A eucharistic congress is an organized public assembly that is designed to manifest faith in the holy Eucharist and often unified by a central theme. Participants include clergy, religious, and laypeople from many countries, as well as representatives of various Catholic organizations. A eucharistic congress consists of meetings and various types of instruction that discuss aspects of eucharistic doctrine and practice. Such congresses also include liturgical services and other public ceremonies.

The origins of the eucharistic congress come from a Frenchwoman, Marie Marthe Emilia Tamisier (1834–1910), who directed her efforts toward encouraging people to visit places where eucharistic miracles had occurred. The first international eucharistic congress took place in 1881 in Lille, France, with the blessing of Pope Leo XIII. Since then, there have been fifty-three international congresses, including the one that took place from September 8 to 15, 2024, in Quito, Ecuador.

International eucharistic congresses are supervised by the Pontifical Committee for International Eucharistic Congresses, while national eucharistic congresses are sponsored at the national and local levels.

Eucharistic Exposition and Benediction

Elevating the host after consecration and the custom of eucharistic processions arose because of the people's desire to see the consecrated host. They were inspired with awe at the self-effacing humility of the Lord of glory and were filled with joy at the sight of this sacramental sign of his abiding presence. Thus began a rich development of various forms of public adoration. One of these popular forms of worship that developed in the Middle Ages is called Benediction of the Blessed Sacrament.

After Vatican II, the Church revised its rite for the service of Benediction, during which those present direct their full attention to the sight of the consecrated host in order to acknowledge the Real Presence of Christ. The purpose of Benediction is to further expand appreciation for the eucharistic mystery and to increase the faithful's desire to participate fully in the Mass, in which the Eucharist is consumed and shared.

Benediction consists of four parts:

1. *Exposition*: The presider approaches the tabernacle and removes the host, placing it in a monstrance, which usually sits on the altar. The presider then uses incense to offer reverence to the Blessed Sacrament.
2. *Adoration*: The Blessed Sacrament remains exposed on the altar, during which time prayers, hymns, Scripture readings, a homily, and silence may occur.
3. *Benediction*: The presider blesses the assembly with the monstrance and says a concluding prayer. The Divine Praises prayer usually concludes Benediction, but it is not a requirement in the revised rite.
4. *Reposition*: This is the final part of the rite, during which the presider removes the Blessed Sacrament from the monstrance and places it back in the tabernacle. In addition to the Divine

Praises, two familiar hymns are traditionally sung by Catholics during Benediction: "O Salutaris Hostia" and "Pange Lingua." However, any suitable eucharistic hymn may be sung.

Holy Hour of Adoration

This eucharistic devotion consists of an hour of prayer in front of the exposed Blessed Sacrament. As a practice, the custom of the Holy Hour draws its inspiration from Christ's admonition to the apostles in Gethsemane: "Could you not keep watch for one hour?" (Mark 14:37).

The devotion of the Holy Hour was taught to St. Margaret Mary Alacoque when our Lord spoke these words to her in June 1674: "Every week between Thursday and Friday, I will grant you a share in that mortal sadness which I chose to feel in the Garden of Olives. You shall keep me company in the prayer I then offered to my Father."

This devotion is one of the special practices associated with devotion to the Sacred Heart. Later in the nineteenth century, a French Jesuit founded a confraternity known as the Archconfraternity of the Holy Hour to help foster this devotion. The Holy Hour devotion has spread to many other countries and is quite popular today.

Perpetual Adoration of the Eucharist

Perpetual adoration is a eucharistic devotion in which people of a particular church, diocese, or religious community practice uninterrupted adoration of the Blessed Sacrament during the day and night, twenty-four hours a day, seven days a week, without end. In some cases, perpetual adoration takes place in a small chapel apart from the main church building.

From a practical standpoint, the concept of perpetual adoration developed out of the Forty Hours devotion. In 1642, Baron de Renty, famous for his devotion to the Blessed Sacrament, founded an association of women in Paris for perpetual adoration. In 1654, the Benedictine nun Mother Mechtilde founded the first community of Benedictines of the Perpetual Adoration of the Blessed Sacrament. Since then, many religious communities have made eucharistic adoration either the main or an essential part of their rule of life.

One of the most famous religious communities founded for such purposes is the Congregation of the Blessed Sacrament, founded in 1856 by St. Peter Julian Eymard. There are several classes of members, including contemplatives consecrated to perpetual adoration and religious who promote devotion to the Eucharist.

The Dicastery for Divine Worship and the Discipline of the Sacraments has ruled that perpetual adoration of the Blessed Sacrament in parishes is allowed by the Church; however, the local bishop has the final say concerning its practice in his diocese. Pope St. John Paul II was a major advocate of eucharistic adoration. He started daily adoration with exposition of the Blessed Sacrament in St. Peter's Basilica and erected a perpetual adoration chapel in Rome at the prompting of Mother Teresa.

Reverence for Viaticum

Through the centuries, the main reason for reservation of the Blessed Sacrament has been prompted by the need for viaticum for the dying. Originally, the Blessed Sacrament was brought to the sick and dying by the priest immediately after the eucharistic celebration. This was done to preserve the connection between the Mass and our Lord's Divine Presence in the host. However, this method has changed over the years. At one time, the Blessed Sacrament was brought either by members of the sick person's family or by a deacon. There were also times when family members were allowed to keep the host reserved in the home so that the sick person could receive Communion explicitly as viaticum as soon as he or she felt death approaching. It has always been a matter of great concern to the Church that the sick have access to viaticum and frequent Communion during long-lasting illness.

As early as the thirteenth century, the faithful, carrying candles, were invited to accompany the Blessed Sacrament from the church to the house of the sick person. This was a popular tradition for some time, but it is not the norm in modern times. The wonderful fact that Jesus remains in the Blessed Sacrament, ever ready to console the sick, should enkindle special devotion, gratitude, and adoration. Receiving the Eucharist as viaticum is also a strong motive to share in Jesus' love for the sick and dying.

If possible, the whole family should gather and welcome the Lord when the Blessed Sacrament is brought to the sick in the home. Great care should be taken that sick people are given the opportunity to receive holy Communion frequently and, especially when in danger of death, receive viaticum while still fully conscious.

In view of the shortage of priests and deacons, qualified laypeople can render valuable service in caring for the lonely and sick through loving care and prayerful assistance. In many Catholic parishes, laypeople are entrusted with this special ministry of bringing the Blessed Sacrament to the sick.

Section Eight

Private Prayers

Here is a selection of prayers suitable for a private visit to the Blessed Sacrament. You can also use these prayers as a model to create prayers of your own.

The Angel's Prayer at Fátima

Most Holy Trinity—Father, Son, and Holy Spirit—I adore you from the depths of my being. I offer you the Body, Blood, Soul, and Divinity of Jesus Christ, present in all the tabernacles of the world, in reparation for the outrages, sacrileges, and indifferences by which he is offended. And through the infinite merits of his most Sacred Heart and the Immaculate Heart of Mary, I ask of you the conversion of all sinners. Amen.

Prayer of St. Faustina Kowalska

I adore you, Lord and Creator, hidden in the most Blessed Sacrament. I adore you for all the works of your hands that reveal to me so much wisdom, goodness, and mercy, O Lord. You have spread so much beauty over the earth, and it tells me about your beauty, even though these things are but a faint reflection of your incomprehensible attraction. And though you have hidden yourself and concealed your beauty, my eye, enlightened by faith, reaches you, and my soul recognizes its Creator, its highest good.

My Lord, your goodness encourages me to converse with you. Your mercy abolishes the chasm which separates the Creator from the creature. You, O Lord, are the delight of my heart. Amen.

Prayer of Bishop Nicholas of Cusa

O Lord, how sweet is your goodness. It is your will that we proclaim your death in the eating of the Bread of Life. What more could you give to us, who deserve to die through the eating of the forbidden fruit than life through the eating of the Bread? O Food of Life, nailed to the cross, who can grasp the bountiful gift which you offer—the gift of your very self as food?

O Food which truly nourishes and satisfies, not our flesh but our soul, not our body but our spirit. O Memorial, worthy to be cherished in our inmost soul, to be deeply engraved on our mind and lovingly preserved in the tabernacle of our heart. Its remembrance is a joy forever and a cause for tears that well up from a heart filled with overpowering joy. Amen.

Prayer of St. John Chrysostom

O Lord, bless those who bless you, and sanctify those who trust in you. Save your people and bless their inheritance, and keep your household, the Church, under your protection. Sanctify those who love the beauty of your house; reward them with glory through your divine power and do not forsake those who hope in you. To the sick give your aid, healing, and comfort. Keep safe all who travel by land or water. Send us seasonable weather and bless the fruits of the earth. Keep peace in the world and among all your people. Grant rest to the departed and remember those who have offered gifts to you. Save those who are in any way afflicted or distressed, and grant us all your heavenly grace. Amen.

Prayer of Pope St. John XXIII

O Jesus, King of all peoples and all ages, accept the acts of adoration and praise which we, your sisters and brothers by adoption, humbly offer you. You are the "living Bread which comes down from heaven and gives life to the world" (John 6:33), Supreme Priest and Victim. On the cross, you offered yourself to the Eternal Father as a bloody sacrifice of expiation, for the redemption of the human race, and now you offer yourself daily upon our altars by the hands of your ministers, in order to establish in every heart your "reign of truth and life, of holiness and grace, of justice, love, and peace" (Preface of Christ the King Mass).

O King of glory, may your kingdom come! Reign from your "throne of grace" (Hebrews 4:16) in our homes, so that parents and children may live in peace in obedience to your holy law. Reign in our land, so that all citizens, in the harmonious order of the various social groups, may feel themselves children of the same heavenly Father, called to cooperate for the common good of this world, happy to belong to the one Mystical Body, of which your sacrament is at once the symbol and everlasting source.

O Jesus, present in the sacrament of the altar, teach all the nations to serve you with willing hearts, knowing that "to serve God is to reign." May your sacrament, O Jesus, be light to the mind, strength to the will, joy to the heart. May it be the support of the weak, the comfort of the suffering, the wayfaring Bread of salvation for the dying, and for all the "pledge of future glory." Amen.

Short Prayers

Jesus, our unfailing source of goodness, friend of our souls, let our prayers knock at your tabernacle door, begging you to open to us, to welcome us, and, through your Blessed Sacrament, to bring to us a favorable answer to every sacred desire of our hearts, through the help of your grace. Amen.

✣

Heart of Jesus, made for love of us, living for love of us, dying for love of us, be always our good friend, consoling us when we visit you, blessing us in your holy Eucharist, and giving yourself to us in holy Communion, so that our hearts, inspired by your great love, may grow in devotion to you, now and to the hour of our deaths. Amen.

✣

May the heart of Jesus in the most Blessed Sacrament be praised, adored, and loved with grateful affection, at every moment, in all the tabernacles of the world, even to the end of time. Amen.